e Reader

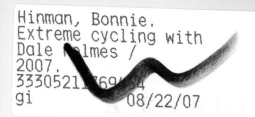

A Robbie Reader

Extreme Cycling with Dale Holmes

Bonnie Hinman

Authorized Biography

Mitchell Lane
PUBLISHERS

P.O. Box 196
Hockessin, Delaware 19707
Visit us on the web: www.mitchelllane.com
Comments? email us: mitchelllane@mitchelllane.com

Mitchell Lane PUBLISHERS

Printing   1   2   3   4   5   6   7   8   9

Extreme Sports
Extreme Cycling with Dale Homes
Extreme Skateboarding with Paul Rodriguez
Ride the Giant Waves with Garrett McNamara
Ultra Running with Scott Jurek

Library of Congress Cataloging-in-Publication Data
Hinman, Bonnie.
    Extreme cycling with Dale Holmes / by Bonnie Hinman.
        p. cm. — (A Robbie reader Extreme sports)
    Includes bibliographical references and index.
    ISBN 1-58415-487-X (library bound : alk. paper)
    1. Holmes, Dale, 1971—Juvenile literature. 2. Cyclists—Juvenile literature. 3. Bicycle motocross—Juvenile literature. 4. Extreme sports—Juvenile literature. I. Title. II. Series.
        GV1051.H66H56 2007
        796.6'2—dc22
                                                                    2006014817

ISBN-10: 1-58415-487-X   ISBN-13: 978-1-58415-487-7

ABOUT THE AUTHOR: Bonnie Hinman has been a writer for over thirty years. Her books for Mitchell Lane Publishers include *Florence Nightingale and the Advancement of Nursing* and *Pennsylvania: William Penn and the City of Brotherly Love*. Her book *A Stranger in His Own House: The Story of W.E.B. Du Bois* (Morgan Reynolds) was chosen for the 2006 New York Public Library's Books for the Teen Age. She lives in Joplin, Missouri, with her husband, Bill, two cats, and three dogs.

PHOTO CREDITS: Cover, pp. 1, 3—Justin Kosman; p. 4—Bart de Jong; pp. 6, 8—Valerie and John Holmes; p. 9—Justin Kosman; p. 10, 12—Valerie and John Holmes; p. 14—Justin Kosman; p. 16—Valerie and John Holmes; pp. 18, 20, 21, 22—Justin Kosman; p. 24—Valerie and John Holmes; pp. 25, 26, 27—Justin Kosman

PUBLISHER'S NOTE: This book has been authorized and approved for print by Dale Holmes. It is based on personal interviews with Dale Holmes conducted by Carol Smalley in October 2005 and Bonnie Hinman in January 2006.

DISCLAIMER: The sport of extreme cycling should not be attempted without extensive training, experience, proper protective gear, and professional assistance. This is both a high risk and dangerous sport and may result in or cause serious injury to oneself or another and may even cause death. Always consult with a trained professional in extreme cycling before trying this sport. Mitchell Lane Publishers shall not be held liable for any injuries to or damages caused by individuals attempting this sport. *Always Put Safety First.*

TABLE OF CONTENTS

*Words in **bold type** can be found in the glossary.

A Robbie Reader

BMX riders sometimes seem to be flying through the air. Dale is airborne as he leads the race at the 2005 UCI World Championships in Paris, France.

WORLD CHAMPION

The gate dropped. Dale Holmes and his bike exploded forward. It was a perfect start, but he found himself behind American Randy Stumpfhauser. The two men pushed their bikes and themselves to the limit as they sped up on the downhill, controlled tightly on the curves, and flew over the jumps. Randy kept the lead as the crowd roared from the sidelines of the outdoor BMX track in Brighton, England.

Dale said later, "The crowd was going nuts. My **adrenaline** (ah-DREH-nuh-len) was surging, but I stayed calm." He waited for just the right time to make his move.

Dale moves ahead of his opponent at the 1993 World Championships in Holland. Concentration is important because the races are short.

Dale had built his whole life that year around training for this race. He had finished second and third before at the BMX World Championships. This time he wanted first or nothing. He knew he would rather crash than come in second.

The weather was great that day, and Dale took one heat, or moto, at a time. "It was a huge accomplishment (ah-KOM-plish-ment) just to make the finals," Dale said. He had made it, but now he was trailing Randy.

Finally the moment came. Randy went slightly wide on the last corner. In an instant Dale saw his chance and went for it. He passed Randy and **sprinted** across the finish line. Dale was the 1996 BMX World Champion racer by less than a yard. The difference in times was mere tenths of a second.

BMX is short for *bicycle **motocross*** (MOH-toh-kros). BMX got its start in California in the late 1960s. Motocross, the racing of motorcycles on dirt tracks, was popular then.

7

Dale is in the lead (far left) as he races at Riverside, California in 1993. He has successfully landed and the others are still in the air after coming over a big bump in the track.

Kids started racing their bikes on the same kind of tracks. Racers pedal furiously around a short track that has bumps, jumps, and berms, which are banked corners.

Dale's win came after many years of racing, but it was just the beginning of his success.

Dale rails around the second turn in Puerto Rico at the 2006 Tropical Challenge. The berms or banked turns require the racers to ride fast and lean sideways.

By age 13, Dale had been riding in races for three years. The next year he had his first big win in the Nationals at Slough, England.

BORN TO RACE

Dale Holmes was born on October 6, 1971, in Derbyshire, England. His parents, Valerie and John, were English. His sister, Rachel, was just a year old when Dale was born.

Dale got his first bike at age four, complete with training wheels. He loved to ride his bike. When he was a little older, he sometimes took an old bike out to ride on rough ground. Soon he was making jumps on dirt bumps.

When Dale was nine, he read a BMX magazine at school. That magazine changed

Dale and his sister, Rachel, display their many trophies. Sports have always held an interest for both of them. Rachel is now a personal trainer in England.

his life. He discovered that the rough rides and jumps he loved to do on his bike had a name— BMX.

Dale got his first BMX bike for Christmas the following year. He rode his first race at age ten in Nottingham, England. He took fourth place.

Dale liked to see his friends at school, but all he really wanted to do was get out of school and ride his bike. **Geography** (jee-AH-grah-fee) interested him, and he liked sports and physical education, but bikes were his life.

Dale's first big racing win was the 1985 National in Slough (SLAU), England, when he was 13. He first raced in the BMX World Championships in 1986, also at Slough.

He graduated from school in England at age 16. For a couple of years he tried different jobs. First he was a carpenter (KAR-pen-ter), and then he worked in engineering (en-jih-NEER-ing). His parents wanted him to study a trade, but all Dale wanted to do was ride a bike.

Finally Dale went to work for his father in the family pub, or restaurant. He split his time between BMX racing and work. He was moving closer to his dream.

Dale puts the pedal to the metal down the first straightaway at the 2006 Tropical Challenge in Puerto Rico. BMX riders sometimes look like they are about to fall off their bikes, but they are in control.

Dale takes a break from ramping the trails at his local hot spot in Murrieta, California. Dale likes to live in California because the weather is better than in England. He can train all winter.

TURNING PRO

Dale began racing for money right after he graduated from school. Earning money for a hobby is called turning professional (proh-FEH-shuh-nul), or turning pro.

Many professional athletes have sponsors. Sponsors often are companies that sell the gear athletes need to compete. Dale and other pro BMX racers are sponsored by bicycle companies and makers of bicycle equipment.

Dale was able to become a full-time racer when he had enough sponsors and was winning enough prize money to support

himself. BMX racing became his job when he
was 19.

Successful (suk-SES-ful) pro BMX racers
have to travel a lot. Dale went from local races
to national races to **international** (in-ter-NAH-
shuh-nul) races. Each year he won more and
more competitions.

BMX racing is **regulated** (REG-yuh-lay-tid)
by several organizations (or-gah-nih-ZAY-shuns).

Dale crouches on his bike as he tries to gain speed
at the 1996 World Championship at Brighton,
England. Dale's tactics worked because he won the
race and became the World Champion.

The American Bicycle Association (ABA) and the National Bicycle League (NBL) are the two main groups in the United States. Union Cycliste International (UCI) is the world organization for all kinds of bicycle racing.

The ABA and NBL hold race events all over the United States, Canada, and Puerto Rico. Other races are held in Europe, Australia, and South America. A race winner earns points, which add up during a racing season. The racers with the most points are **ranked** and get invited to the best events with the highest prize money.

Some years Dale travels to 35 different race events all over the world. In one weekend race event, he might race 20 times. Meanwhile he still has to train. It hasn't been an easy life, but he loves riding and winning.

All Dale's work led up to the exciting weekend in Brighton. The 1996 World Champion celebrated with friends and family, but then it was time to think about his next step.

Dale dives into the third turn at the Nellis BMX track for the 2005 Silver State National Championships in Nevada. A BMX racer doesn't always stay seated as he rides. Sometimes he finds himself touching only the grips and the pedals.

THE BIG MOVE

As Dale became more successful in the early 1990s, he realized that he needed to live in the United States. More races were held there, and the prize money was better. After he won the world championship at Brighton in 1996, he decided to move to Huntington Beach, California.

Dale continued to win races all over the world. His list of honors includes British Champion, European Champion, and UCI World Cup Champion. He was the number one ranked BMX racer in the world in 1997 and

1998. In 2001 at the UCI World Championships in Louisville, Kentucky, Dale won the top award again.

Dale lives in California but goes back to England four or five times a year to race and see his family. While he's there, he also makes appearances to advertise for his sponsors.

An important part of Dale's winning **strategy** (STRAA-teh-jee) has been his training. BMX races are short, but they are **intense** and physically hard. A racer like Dale has to keep his body in top shape to compete. Dale trains almost every day he isn't racing.

After breakfast he heads to the gym to lift weights. Some days he goes for long-distance rides on a 10-speed or mountain bike. In the evenings he usually

Dale hangs out with his fellow BMX racers. From left to right: Derek Betcher, Kyle Bennett, Greg Romero, and Dale. They often compete against each other but are still good friends.

goes to the local BMX track to practice starts and skills.

Dale is careful to eat a healthy diet all the time. He eats lots of pasta, different kinds of protein, and vegetables.

For fun, Dale likes to hang out with his racing friends. They watch other sports, but most of the time talk is about BMX racing and the next big event.

Dale relaxes for a minute while training in 2006. He trains every day that he isn't racing or traveling. He always wears gloves and a helmet in case he falls.

ON TO THE OLYMPICS

Dale turned 35 in 2006, and that sometimes earns him the title of Old Man at the BMX racetracks. Most BMX racers are younger than Dale. That doesn't mean that he intends to retire any time soon. He has a few more goals he wants to reach first.

He would like to win another world championship. The biggest goal of all is to represent Britain at the Olympics in Beijing (bay-JIN), China, in 2008. This will be the first time that BMX racing has been an Olympic sport. Dale is working hard to make the British team.

Every world-class athlete dreams of standing on the **podium** (POH-dee-um) at the Olympics, accepting a gold medal for his or her country. Dale has that dream, too.

Dale also wants to get a little better each year. The courses get harder and the competition stiffer as each season unfolds.

In 2006 he accepted a job as manager for a new Free Agent World Team. Dale has **recruited** (ree-KROO-tid) racers from several

Dale (center) takes the podium after winning the European championships in Holland in 1997.

Dale leads a pack of pro riders through the first turn at the 2005 Silver State National Championship in Nellis, Nevada. Pro riders travel all over the world to race.

countries to make up the team. They will compete in events all around the world.

Dale knows that younger riders look up to professional racers. There's usually a crowd of young bikers around every pro rider. To help

Dale practices jumping, an important skill in racing. Training isn't always done on a bike. There are other ways to help keep your body strong and able to win races.

set a good example, Dale and other Free Agent World Team members will be holding a series of clinics for riders all over the United States.

"If you want to be a BMX racer," Dale says, "start small. Jumping is important, but start with jumping off curbs. Then move up to bigger jumps."

Dale says, "Extreme biking is something you do for yourself. It's all about you and your bike."

It follows that the better you know your bike and your own skills and limits, the faster you can race. And winning races is what BMX racing is all about.

CHRONOLOGY

1971   Born October 6 in Derbyshire, England

1976   Gets first bicycle at age four

1981   Rides in first BMX race in Nottingham, England

1985   First big win at Nationals in Slough, England

1988   Graduates from secondary school; turns pro

1996   Wins World Championships in Brighton, England

1997   Is ranked number one in world (also in 1998); moves to United States

2001   Wins World Championships in Louisville, Kentucky

2002   Free Agent Bicycles becomes his sponsor

2003   Is oldest rider ever to win American Nationals (Reno, Nevada)

2006   Is made manager of Free Agent World Team; begins training for the 2008 Olympics

GLOSSARY

adrenaline (ah-DREH-nuh-len)—A substance made by the body that can make a person feel stronger.

geography (jee-AH-grah-fee)—The study of the earth's surface and how everything on it works together.

intense (in-TENS)—Very strong.

international (in-ter-NAH-shuh-nul)—Involving two or more countries.

motocross (MOH-toh-kros)—A race over a closed course of rough terrain, including mud, bumps, hills, and hairpin turns.

podium (POH-dee-um)—A low platform.

ranked (RANKD)—Put in an order.

recruited (ree-KROO-tid)—Convinced to join.

regulate (REG-yuh-layt)—To organize and oversee, making sure certain rules are followed.

sprinted (SPRIN-tid)—Went a short distance at top speed.

strategy (STRAA-teh-jee)—A plan of actions to reach a goal.

FIND OUT MORE

Books

Bishop, Amanda, and Bobbie Kahlman. *Extreme Sports No Limits: Extreme BMX.* New York: Crabtree Publishing Company, 2004.

Gutman, Bill. *BMX Racing.* Mankato, Minnesota: Capstone Books, 1995.

Gutman, Bill, and Shawn Frederick. *Catching Air.* New York: Citadel Press, 2004.

Herran, Joe, and Ron Thomas. *BMX Riding.* Philadelphia: Chelsea House Publishers, 2003.

Maurer, Tracy Nelson. *BMX Freestyle.* Vero Beach, Florida: Rourke Publications, 2002.

Nelson, Julie. *BMX Racing and Freestyle.* Austin, Texas: Steadwell Books, 2002.

Partland, J.P., and Tony Donaldson. *The World of BMX.* St. Paul, Minnesota: MBI Publishing Company, 2003.

Peters, Stephanie. *Matt Christopher: The Extreme Team #7: Wild Ride.* Washington D.C.: National Geographic, 2002.

Works Consulted

"ABA Worlds," *BMX Plus!,* November 2005, Volume 28, Issue 11, pp. 26–35.

"Ask the BMX Experts," *BMX Plus!,* March 2006, Volume 29, Issue 3, pp. 16–17.

"Getting Started in Racing," *BMX Plus!,* October 2005, Volume 28, Issue 10, pp. 68–72.

Hinman, Bonnie. Personal interview with Dale Holmes, January 23, 2006.

"Interview with *Nirves'* Dale Holmes," October 27, 2000, http://www.bmxultra.com/prosection/interview/daleholmes.htm

"Pro Spotlight: Dale Holmes," 2003, http://bmxpros.com/dalehfeature.htm

"Safe Helmet," *BMX Plus!,* November 2005, Volume 28, Issue 11, pp. 46–51.

Schuman, Matt. "BMX Camp," *Greeley [Colorado] Tribune,* August 11, 2005.

Smalley, Carol Parenzan. Personal interview with Dale Holmes, October 20, 2005.

Zielinski, Jeff. "If You Build It, They Will Come," *Ride BMX,* January 2006, Volume 15.

On the Internet

BMX Mania
http://www.bmxmania.com

BMXWORLD Magazine
http://www.bmxworldmag.com

Free Agent World Team
http://www.freeagentbmx.com/

Official Web Site of British Cycling
http://www.britishcycling.org.uk

Official Web Site of Dale Holmes
http://www.daleholmes.com

INDEX